YOU PICK HISTORY

Could You Survive Ancient Greece?

First published in Great Britain in 2026 by Red Shed, part of Farshore

Text adapted from *Would You Rather? Ancient Greeks*,
published 2024 by Red Shed
An imprint of HarperCollins*Publishers*
1 London Bridge Street, London SE1 9GF
www.farshore.co.uk

HarperCollins*Publishers*
Macken House, 39/40 Mayor Street Upper, Dublin 1, D01 C9W8, Ireland

ISBN 978 0 00 883789 1
Printed in Malaysia.
1

A CIP catalogue record for this title is available from the British Library.

YOU PICK HISTORY

COULD YOU SURVIVE ANCIENT GREECE?

CLIVE GIFFORD
TIM WESSON

RED SHED

WELCOME TO
ANCIENT GREECE!

Hello – or **Χαίρετε**, as they said in ancient Greek! This incredible civilization invented catapults, cheesecake (yum), theatre, the Olympics, showers and the yo-yo – and that's not all. The Greeks were BIG thinkers and made developments in philosophy, maths and engineering, and created systems we still use today, like democracy and trials by jury.

So when did it all get started? There have been people in the area we know today as Greece for thousands of years. The Minoan civilization got going on the island of Crete around a whopping 4,000 years ago, and the Mycenaean Greeks were there until the 1400s BCE. But it wasn't until around 800BCE that the ancient Greeks we know and love began to flourish.

Greece wasn't one big empire, like the Roman Empire, or a single kingdom like ancient Egypt. Instead, the ancient Greek world was made up of lots of smaller city-states spread around the mainland and islands of Greece and beyond, such as Athens, Sparta and Olympia. See if you can spot all three on the map opposite. They didn't always get on, and wars kept their armies and navies nice and busy.

For a few centuries, ancient Greece was THE place to be. It had grand temples and palaces, poetry and powerful military forces. Super-bright minds flocked to the region and pushed knowledge forward.

In this book, you will go on a spectacular adventure back in time, to discover more about what life was *really* like in ancient Greece, from games and gods to myths and jobs.

Get ready to pick what YOUR ancient Greek life would look like – and find out some hot tips for surviving to tell the tale.

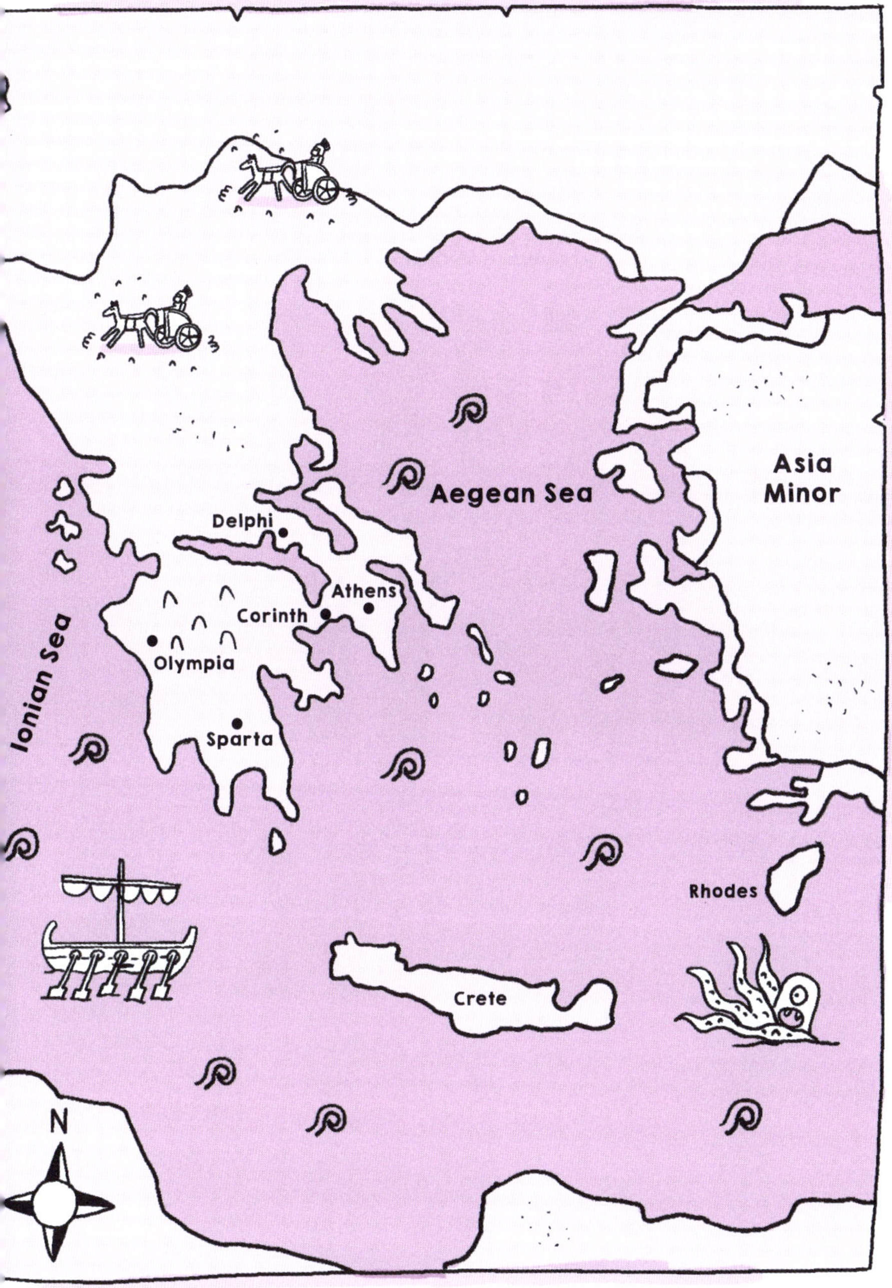
Aegean Sea
Asia Minor
Delphi
Athens
Corinth
Olympia
Sparta
Ionian Sea
Rhodes
Crete
N

HOW TO USE THIS BOOK

Each page has some brilliant facts and information about ancient Greek life. All you have to do is read what's there, then make a decision. Such as . . .

Could you survive a life of stealing cabbages?

Could you stay on the good side of Poseidon, god of the sea?

Could you make it out of an ancient Greek wrestling match alive?

As you go, you will be directed to different pages, each with new choices to make. Keep going for as long as you like, and discover if you would survive ancient Greece! If you feel like choosing a different path, simply go back to the beginning and start again.

Are you ready to start living your best ancient Greek life? Grab your sandals and turn the page for your first ancient Greek survival challenge . . .

BE A TYRANT

If you think that being in charge rules, this might be the role for you!

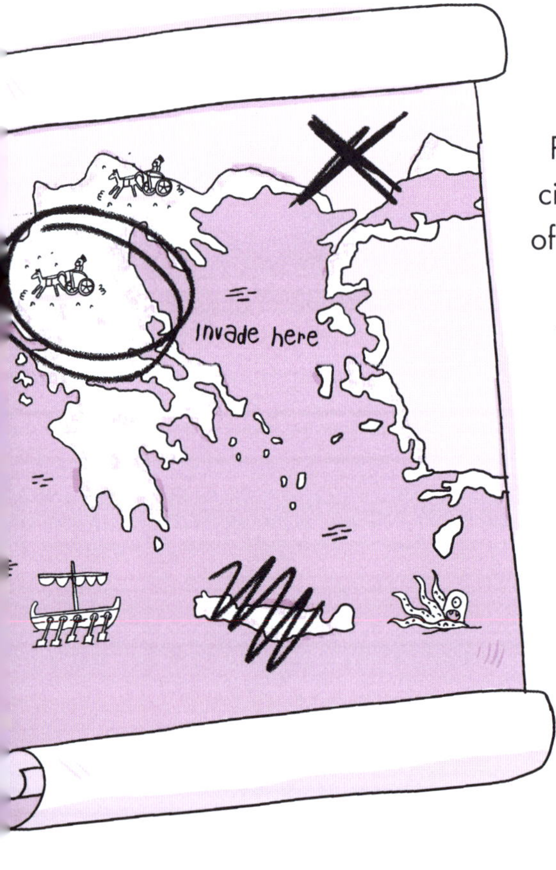

Job description

Pick an ancient Greek city-state to take control of – then gather an army, sweep in and make yourself the sole ruler!

Perks of the job

- Absolute power!
- Popularity – tyrants were often popular with the people because of the changes they made, such as creating jobs or building temples.

Downsides of the job

- Your army might turn against you.
- If you bumped off a popular figure or introduced harsh laws or taxes, you might not be a tyrant for long.

Who knew?

Some Greek city-states were run by tyrants, but others were run differently – for example, some had a king or powerful family in charge.

COULD YOU SURVIVE AS A TYRANT?

YES!

Sounds like you need a bigger challenge! Go to **page 22** to be king of the gods.

NO!

Ruling's not for everyone. Go to **page 38** to become a hoplite soldier.

BE AN OLYMPIAN

Do you dream of fame and glory? How about becoming a celebrated ancient Olympic athlete?

Job description

Greek athletes had all sorts of skills: running, throwing, jumping, chariot driving, wrestling and much more. Take your pick!

Perks of the job

Winners might be given money or property by the city-state they represented. Some champions from Athens even got free meals for life. Yum!

Fair play

Competitors had to swear an oath in front of a statue of Zeus to say they would compete fairly.

Downsides of the job

- The training to get ready for the games was hard work.
- Athletes who were caught cheating could face a whipping.
- Most athletes took part nude!

The ancient Olympic games started in 776BCE in the city-state of Olympia. They went on for around 1,000 years.

WOULD YOU PICK AN ATHLETE'S LIFE?

YES!

Great! Broaden your sporting skills as a wrestler on **page 70**.

NO!

Sport isn't all about the athletes. Go to **page 42** to try being a sweat scraper.

GO TO THE TOILET

We've all got to do it . . . but how would you get on in an ancient Greek bathroom?

Live like a Greek

The Greeks invented what may well have been the very first flushing toilet! It was installed in a small room in the Palace of Knossos on the island of Crete.

The Palace of Knossos was built around 1900BCE – that's around 2,000 years before the Romans built the Colosseum!

How did it work?

The toilet at Knossos was attached to a special channel, built below the room the toilet was in. After they had done their business, the visitor used a jug of water to flush the waste into the channel, where it could flow away. Easy *pee-sy*.

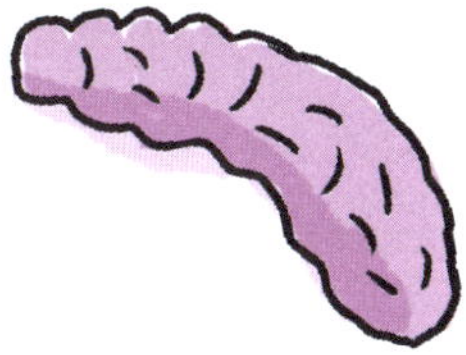

To ~~do~~ poo list

- Bring pessoi. These were pebbles or pieces of broken pottery used for wiping. Ouch!
- Don't forget a chamber pot. Many ancient Greeks brought their own portable pot to parties for when they needed the loo.

WOULD YOU USE AN ANCIENT GREEK TOILET?

YES!

Great! You're living like a Greek! Go to **page 76** to find out more about home life in Athens.

NO!

Fancy something different? Try playing a game on **page 26**.

BE A SPARTAN WOMAN

Do you love PE? Life in the city-state of Sparta might be perfect for you!

Spartan life

Sparta was BIG on sport and exercise. Women in this city-state practised sports such as running and wrestling.

Why all the exercise? Spartans thought that strong women would have healthier children.

The good bits

Unlike many women in history, Spartan women could own land and property, and took charge of running the family business if their husband went off to war (which was often).

Look like a Spartan

- Women wore a *peplos* – a wool dress worn with a belt around the waist.
- When Spartan women got married, it was traditional for their heads to be shaved.

WOULD YOU SURVIVE AS A SPARTAN WOMAN?

YES!
Brilliant! Spartans loved a party.
Go to **page 36** to find out more.

NO!
Try being an Athenian instead.
Go to **page 76**.

BE KING OF THE GODS

Do you love bossing people about? Have a go at being Zeus – ruler of the Greek gods!

Character traits

Hot-headed and harsh. When one character called Prometheus annoyed Zeus by giving humans the gift of fire, he was chained to a rock where eagles ate his liver. Ouch.

Worst enemies

His wife, Hera. Zeus had many girlfriends, which made Hera extremely cross.

Specialist subjects

- Thunder and lightning (and weather generally)
- Fate
- Law and order

Who knew?

Zeus was a protector of cities, property, strangers and guests.

COULD YOU RULE THE GODS?

YES!
How about the Underworld? Go to **page 72**.

NO!
Not everyone can be king. Take on the sea god Poseidon on **page 40**.

Powerful weapons

Zeus carried thunderbolts that he could throw with deadly accuracy. Spare thunderbolts were carried by his winged horse, Pegasus.

JOB VACANCY

ORACLE

JOB DESCRIPTION

Oracles were priestesses whose main job was talking directly with the gods, then delivering prophecies (reports of what the gods say will happen). To speak with the gods they would enter a trance state – a kind of deep daydream where they were unaware of the people around them.

PERKS OF THE JOB

- An oracle's word was never doubted (even if the prophecy was vague).
- You could be famous! People would flock to an oracle's temple to hear their wisdom.
- Spa access – in between doling out predictions, oracles would bathe in holy pools to purify themselves.

DOWNSIDES

- The oracle at Delphi had to give up her life to serve the god Apollo and could never marry.
- They may have breathed in dangerous gases to get themselves into a trance.

WOULD YOU SIGN UP TO BE AN ORACLE?

YES! Better get chatting to the gods and goddesses! Go to **page 32** to meet Athena.

NO! It's not for everyone. Try being a merchant on **page 52**.

NOW SHOWING
SOPHOCLES'

ANTIGONE

"This tragedy is a tearjerker!"

★★★★★

WANTED

Experienced dog walker

VERY IMPORTANT: Must be able to handle multiple dogs

Call now: 248 31226

GET YOUR TEMPLE SUPER SPARKLY!
USE

ORACLE CLEAN

The Sirens

LIVE

AT THE ATHENS ARENA

★★★★★★

WITH SUPPORT FROM THE GORGON SISTERS

BANISH BOREDOM

Do you love games? Good choice! Here's how to play *ephedrismos*, a popular ancient Greek game.

STEP 1

Find a friend to play with.

STEP 2

Fetch a stone that can be knocked over, and stand it on the ground.

STEP 3

Take it in turns to throw another stone from the same distance, and try to knock over the first stone.

STEP 4

Whoever knocks over the first stone is the winner. The loser has to give the winner a piggyback while blindfolded.

STEP 5

The loser tries to touch the knocked-over stone.

FEELING ENTERTAINED?

YES!
Hooray! For another game, go to **page 56**.

NO!
Maybe quizzes are more your thing? Go to **page 58**.

VISIT A DOCTOR

Pick an illness to discover your treatment – hope you're not too squeamish . . .

Fever

Ancient Greeks thought the body could build up too much blood, causing health problems. So, they would cut into an arm or leg and let plenty of blood flow out!

It was possible to become an ancient Greek doctor with next to no training.

Slipped disc

To treat this painful spine condition, an ancient Greek doctor might jump up and down on your back!

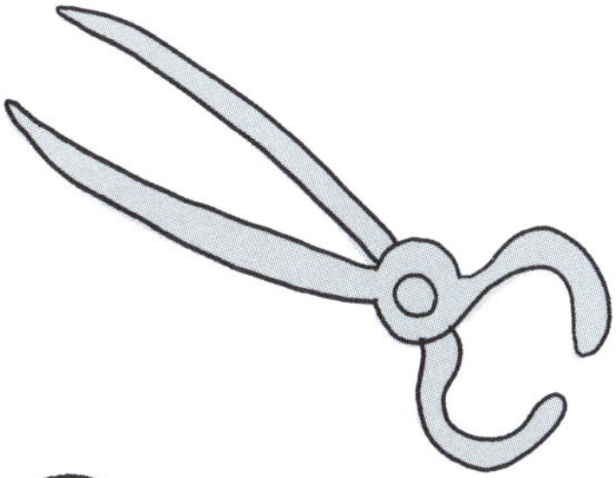

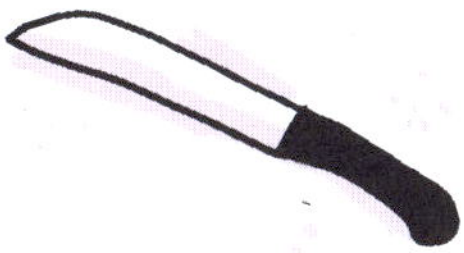

Last resort . . .

If nothing else worked, doctors might try surgery – without anaesthetic to put you to sleep. Ow!

WOULD YOU SURVIVE A TRIP TO THE DOCTOR?

YES!

Phew! Turn to **page 30** to try being a doctor.

NO!

Oops. It's the end of your ancient Greek road. Go to **page 114**.

BE A DOCTOR

Want to become a doctor yourself?

HIPPOCRATES

BORN: 460BCE, Island of Kos

OCCUPATION: Doctor

FACT FILE

- Hippocrates was one of the first doctors who thought that there were natural causes behind bad health. Many others at the time thought their health was down to the gods!
- He thought the body had four humours – blood, phlegm, black bile and yellow bile – and that health problems could happen if these became unbalanced.

What did he do?

He came up with new methods of treating illness – some more effective than others! He often prescribed changes to diet and insisted that the new doctors he trained kept patient records.

Hippocrates used ingredients such as honey, wine, garlic and vinegar in his treatments.

Hippocrates' top tip

Don't be afraid to sniff patients' sweat, spit and wee – or taste their poo, snot, vomit or pus!

WOULD YOU SURVIVE AS AN ANCIENT GREEK DOCTOR?

YES!

Go to **page 112** to reward yourself for your hard work.

NO!

How about some maths instead? Meet up with Archimedes on **page 88**.

FIGHT THE GODDESS OF WAR

Are you cunning, crafty and good in a fight? Try taking on Athena.

Character traits

Good at fighting and extremely competitive! She could be kind and wise . . . or vengeful and unforgiving.

Specialist subjects

- War tactics
- Wisdom
- Weaving
- Pottery

One of Athena's symbols was an owl – a symbol of wisdom.

Who knew?

The city of Athens takes its name from Athena. She and Poseidon competed to make the city theirs by offering the city-dwellers gifts – Athena's gift of an olive tree won! This was said to be the first olive tree – a valuable source of wood and oil.

Worst enemies

Athena usually took revenge on her enemies quickly. When she lost a weaving contest against a skilful woman called Arachne, she turned her into a spider. Eek!

COULD YOU SURVIVE AS ATHENA'S ENEMY?

YES!

You're clearly a hero! Turn to **page 34** to pick your name.

NO!

Get to know Hermes instead on **page 62**.

PICK YOUR GREEK EPITHET

Heroes in ancient Greek mythology were often given epithets – nicknames related to their special skills. Achilles, known as one of the strongest warriors in Greek myth, had lots, including 'Achilles the Lion-hearted'. What would yours be? Choose for yourself below.

Part 1 – Your first name!

Part 2 – The day of your birth

1. The Bold
2. The Strong
3. The Loud
4. The Chatty
5. The Quick
6. The Wise
7. The Bright
8. The Swift
9. The Short
10. The Grumbly
11. The Caring
12. The Smelly
13. The Happy
14. The Stubbornly

15. The Imaginative
16. The Gloomy
17. The Rosy
18. The Dull
19. The Flaky
20. The Delightfully
21. The Serious
22. The Jazzy
23. The Fast
24. The Curious
25. The Modest
26. The Delicious
27. The Powerful
28. The Lively
29. The Mean
30. The Whacky
31. The Jolly

Part 3 – Your birth month

January: -hearted
February: -witted
March: -laughed
April: -minded
May: -socked
June: -spoken
July: -eyed
August: -footed
September: -spirited
October: -tempered
November: -natured
December: -nosed

To meet another hero, go to page 66 – or turn to page 36 to continue your adventure.

ATTEND A FESTIVAL

Forget big stages, famous bands and burger vans – Greek festivals were held by city-states to honour the gods! Could you survive an ancient Greek party?

Anthestaria – Athens

This three-day party honoured the god of wine-making and partying, Dionysus. People smeared tar on their doors to keep the souls of the dead from attacking them. Creepy!

Hybristica – Argos

This festival was dedicated to Aphrodite, goddess of love. It saw men and women swap clothes and roles.

Some cities held a LOT of festivals. Athens alone had around 120 each year!

Carneia – Sparta

Get ready to run! In this festival, boys would chase a man wearing garlands of flowers. If they caught him, it was thought to bring good luck.

WOULD YOU GO TO A GREEK FESTIVAL?

YES!
You've celebrated her festival – now meet Aphrodite herself on **page 110**.

NO!
Try a different part of Greek culture – acting! Go to **page 44**.

BE A HOPLITE SOLDIER

Ready to go into battle? Forward, march!

Job description

Be good at marching, wielding weapons and fighting!

Perks of the job

Hoplites didn't have to worry about spending time alone . . . they fought in a tight formation called a *phalanx*, where they stood shoulder to shoulder with shields overlapping.

The *phalanx* formation was excellent protection – as long as you didn't break free from the ranks!

Who knew?

Hoplites were named after the *hoplon* – a heavy, round wooden shield covered in bronze that each soldier carried.

Drawbacks of the job

- It would get SMELLY. Hoplites would spend a lot of time huddled up together – and there was no deodorant in ancient Greece!
- The risk of being killed was high, as you'd spend a lot of time in battle.

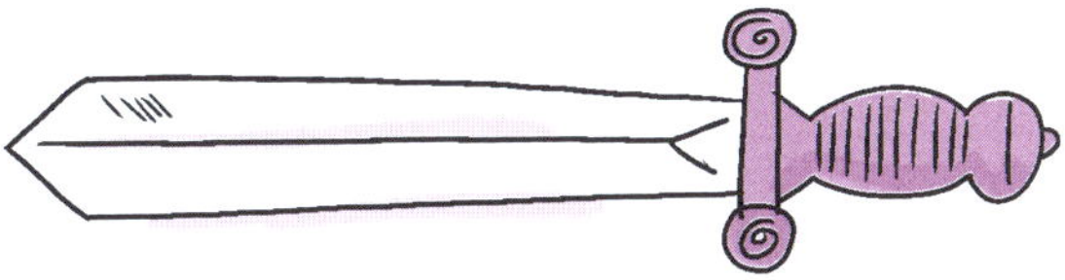

WOULD YOU SURVIVE AS A SOLDIER?

YES!
How about fighting at sea? Go to **page 86**.

NO!
Try a more peaceful life as a priest. Go to **page 64**.

TAKE ON THE GOD OF THE SEA

Nice to 'sea' you – could you survive a battle with Poseidon, ancient Greece's ocean god?

Character traits

Easy to anger (a bit like his brother Zeus). If he blew his top, so did the seas – *wave* hello to huge thunderstorms! He could even cause earthquakes with the trident he carried.

Specialist subjects

- The sea
- Earthquakes
- Horses

Who knew?

Poseidon had many children including the god Triton who was half-man, half-fish, and a sea monster called Charybdis who created giant whirlpools to suck ships underwater.

Competitions

Poseidon often battled with other gods . . . and lost. Hera beat him in a contest to be god of Argos – and Athena did the same over Athens.

COULD YOU WIN A BATTLE WITH POSEIDON?

YES!

Stay at sea with mythological hero Odysseus on **page 74**.

NO!

Go to dry land and meet the sorceress Circe on **page 84**.

BE A SWEAT SCRAPER

If being an ancient Greek personal trainer (known as a *paidotribe*) sounds like fun, you're in the right place.

Job description

Training elite athletes! You'd also massage their huge muscles with olive oil. But where does sweat scraping come in, you ask? Read on . . .

Sweaty situation

Because the ancient Greeks didn't have soap, you'd need to clean the athletes by scraping off the oil, sweat and dirt on their bodies with a special instrument called a *strigil*. Yuck!

Who knew?

The gunky mess of oil, sweat and irt was called *gloios*. Trainers would sell it as medicine. Many people hought it relieved aches and pains!

COULD YOU SURVIVE SCRAPING ATHLETES' SWEAT?

YES!

Ready to get to know one of the strongest Greeks of all? Meet Heracles on **page 66**.

NO!

Philosophy might be less stinky – meet great Greek thinker Aristotle on **page 102**.

ACT IN A PLAY

Time to perform in some of the most celebrated plays of all time! Could you make it as a theatre performer?

Only men acted in plays – bad luck, Greek girls!

Who knew?

Ancient Greek theatre was performed in a *théatron*, meaning a 'place for viewing'. Some of these were huge, holding around 20,000 spectators!

What's involved?

Learn your lines and perform in plays! Most actors were part of a big group of men called the chorus, who all spoke, sang and danced together in a flat part of the *théatron* known as the orchestra.

Turn the page to find out more . . .

Perks of the job

Acting was pretty easy – actors carried masks with different facial expressions. Some were double-sided, so they could flip from happy to sad in an instant.

Plays were sometimes comedies about everyday life, sometimes serious tragedies. Some are still performed in theatres today!

Drawbacks of the job

- Some Greek plays went on for a loooong time. Some could last all day.
- You might need a head for heights. Playwright Euripides introduced a special crane that could hoist actors up and down above the stage!

COULD YOU BE A GREEK ACTOR?

YES!

Better get reading your lines! Meet playwright Aeschylus on **page 108**.

NO!

Try being a market trader on **page 82**.

KEEP HESTIA HAPPY

Hestia was one of ancient Greece's most important goddesses! Could you keep on her good side?

Character traits

Unlike many other gods and goddesses, Hestia was calm, level-headed and humble. As goddess of the home, she also got some great perks . . .

. . . she was often given the first and last portion of ritual meals. Result!

Specialist subjects

- Homes
- Families
- The hearth (a fireplace used for cooking)
- Fire (Hestia looked after the hearth on Mount Olympus, home of the gods. A never-ending, scorching hot task!)

Poseidon and Apollo both wanted to marry Hestia, but she said no to both of them!

Who knew?

Every Greek city had at least one temple or shrine dedicated to Hestia. A fire would be lit there in her honour and never allowed to go out.

WOULD YOU MAKE AN OFFERING TO HESTIA?

YES!

Find out more about life at home on **page 76**.

NO!

If adventure is more your thing, go to **page 86** for some sailing.

BE A PHILOSOPHER

Could you survive a life of logic?

Ask an expert . . .

SOCRATES

BORN: 470BCE, Athens

OCCUPATION: Philosopher

FACT FILE

- Socrates didn't write books – we know about his ideas because other writers recorded them.
- Socrates' main belief was that he knew nothing – he approached everything with an open mind.
- Socrates upset the rulers of Athens so much that he was sentenced to death – by being poisoned. Ouch!

What did he do?

Socrates invented new ways to think about the world. He would wander the streets of Athens, talking with people about the meaning of things like fairness – whether they wanted to or not.

COULD YOU THINK YOUR WAY TO SUCCESS IN ANCIENT GREECE?

YES!

Go to **page 102** to meet another philosopher.

NO!

Spend some time with a hero instead on **page 94**.

JOB VACANCY

MERCHANT

JOB DESCRIPTION

Pack your bags – you'd be sailing out to transport goods to different city-states to sell!

PERKS OF THE JOB

If you picked the right deals, you could make a big, juicy profit. You'd also get to travel a lot and meet different people on the way.

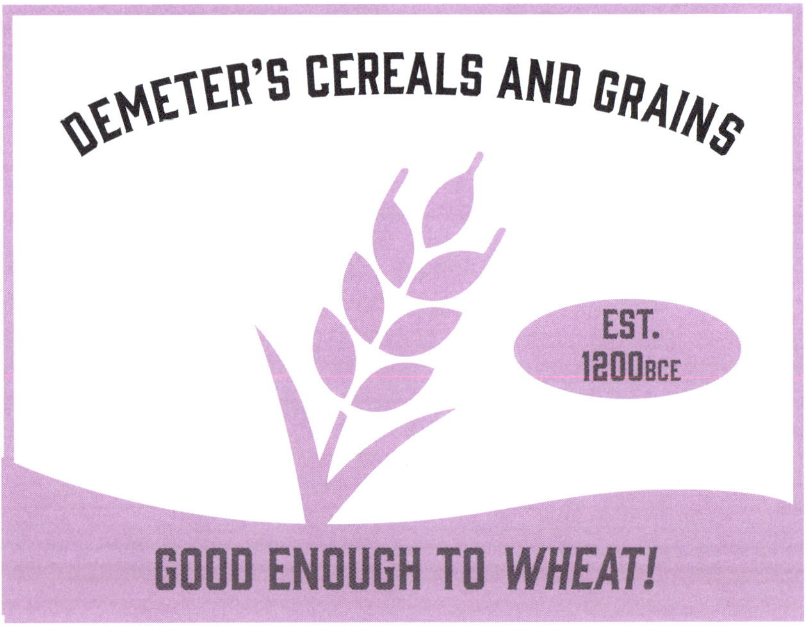

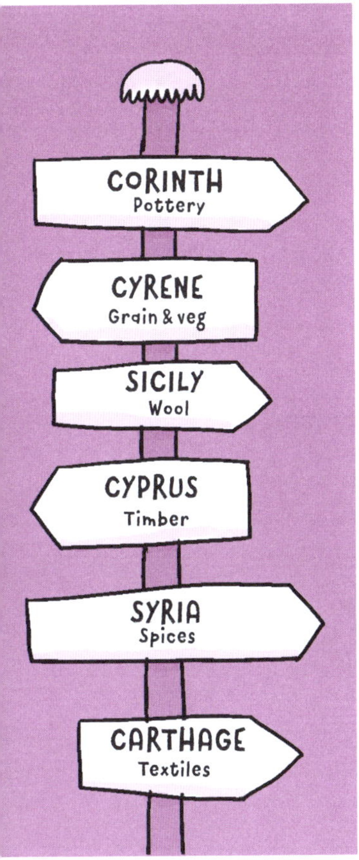

DOWNSIDES

Some traders had to borrow from money-lenders to buy their stock – these lenders might ask for double their money back later on!

TURN OVER FOR MORE

TRADER'S TO DO LIST
Haggle with pesky suppliers
fix hole in ship to avoid soggy stock
Fill ship with goods to trade
Avoid storms
(and pirates!)

Commonly traded goods included olive oil, wine, cheeses, figs, honey, knives, perfume and fine pottery.

MORE DOWNSIDES

- Dangerous seas – ships could be tossed and turned by sudden storms. Once merchants had bought their precious cargo, getting it home safely to sell could be a challenge.
- Pirates – merchants would need to watch out for sneaky attackers waiting to loot their boats!

COULD YOU MAKE A PROFIT AS A MERCHANT?

YES! Try selling your wares as a market trader on **page 82**.

NO! Try stealing instead. Go to **page 98**.

PLAY A BALL GAME

Welcome to *episkyros* – an ancient Greek ball game a bit like rugby! Could you make it to the end?

The pitch

Two teams of around 12–14 players would gather on a pitch with three lines on it – one at each team's end and one down the middle.

Aim of the game

Each team would pass the ball around the pitch, aiming to get the ball behind the opposite team's line.

Look out . . .

This game could get violent – especially in Sparta, known for its tough players. And remember, there were no shin pads or helmets!

COULD YOU SURVIVE AN *EPISKYROS* MATCH?

YES!
Give wrestling a go next on **page 70**.

NO!
Go back to **page 26** for a different game.

SURVIVE THE LEGEND!

Answer these questions to see what sort of character from ancient Greek mythology you'd be . . . and if you'd survive!

1. You have annoyed the goddess Athena. What do you do?

a) Make a sacrifice in her honour.

b) Do nothing. How much can she do anyway?

c) Run away to a remote island – hopefully she'll never notice.

2. You can choose a skill. What is it?

a) Playing the world's most beautiful music.

b) Being good at fighting.

c) Having magical healing powers.

3. A nearby monster is about to devour a princess. What do you do?

a) Run over as quickly as possible to save her.
b) Leave the princess to be eaten.
c) Brew a magic potion to bewitch the monster.

4. You learn a secret from a god. What do you do?

a) Keep it to yourself.
b) Immediately gossip to your friends.
c) Tell just one (carefully chosen) other god.

If you got . . .

Mostly As – HERO. You are a classic hero who survives with their skill and good judgement. Go to **page 94** to meet a hero like you.

Mostly Bs – WARRIOR. You manage to annoy the gods and die an early death. Go to **page 114**.

Mostly Cs – SORCERER. Your cunning ways might just help you survive. Go to **page 84** to meet Circe, a fellow sorcerer.

JOB VACANCY

SLAVE

JOB DESCRIPTION

Whatever your owner wants you to do – in their home, for their business or on their farmland or vineyards.

Some slave jobs

- Farming
- Cooking
- Mining
- Crafts
- Police work
- Luggage carrying
- Quarrying stone
- Digging wells
- Serving rich families

PERKS OF THE JOB

- You'd get fed (a bit).
- Slaves were occasionally freed by their owners.

DOWNSIDES

- You could get beaten whenever your owner fancied it.
- You had no rights.
- You could be given to a new owner at any moment – who might be even meaner!

COULD YOU SURVIVE SLAVE LIFE?

YES! You're DEFINITELY made of strong stuff. Turn to **page 66** to meet a similarly tough Greek hero.

NO! To try some different (and paid!) work, try being a market trader on **page 82**.

PTOLEMY'S POTS
1 COIN
SMASHING PRICES

- IT'S NEW! -
IT'S COINS!
EASY TO CARRY
Buy food, goods and more!
EASY TO USE!
Established in Lydia

RACE DAY
BE QUICK – SIGN UP NOW!
PLACES RUNNING OUT FAST
MARATHON

JOKE WITH HERMES

If you love practical jokes, Hermes is the god for you! Just try not to get on his bad side . . .

Character traits

Massive prankster. Hermes was also speedy – he had winged sandals for making a quick getaway!

Worst enemies

People and gods he annoyed with his pranks – such as the mighty musical god Apollo. When Hermes stole Apollo's cattle, it looked like he was in BIG trouble . . . but then he gifted Apollo a lyre (a stringed musical instrument), and escaped unharmed.

pecialist subjects

- Carrying messages – helped by his winged sandals.
- Travellers and roads.
- Trade – and thieves!

Who knew?

Hermes was said to have travelled to the human realm where he invented the alphabet, dice and mathematics.

Beyond a joke

Hermes was serious about many things. When a nymph called Chelone refused an invitation he delivered, he turned her into a tortoise as punishment!

COULD YOU SURVIVE HERMES' PRANKS?

YES!

Help Hermes take a message to the Underworld!

Go to **page 72**.

NO!

Meet the goddess of love on **page 110**.

JOB VACANCY

PRIEST/ PRIESTESS

JOB DESCRIPTION

You'd be in charge of running a temple and leading all the events and rituals held there. These might include festivals, processions or even animal sacrifices!

PERKS OF THE JOB

- Big respect! Priests and priestesses were valued members of ancient Greek society.
- Priests and priestesses would often receive a decent portion of meat or animal skin from sacrifices as a fee.

DOWNSIDES

- Sacrifices! Priests and priestesses couldn't be squeamish about blood and guts.
- Cleaning! This job involved keeping the temple tidy (including cleaning up all that sacrificial blood).

WOULD YOU SIGN UP TO BE A PRIEST OR PRIESTESS?

YES! Go back to **page 24** and build your priestess skills as an oracle.

NO! Go to **page 82** to try your hand at a completely different job.

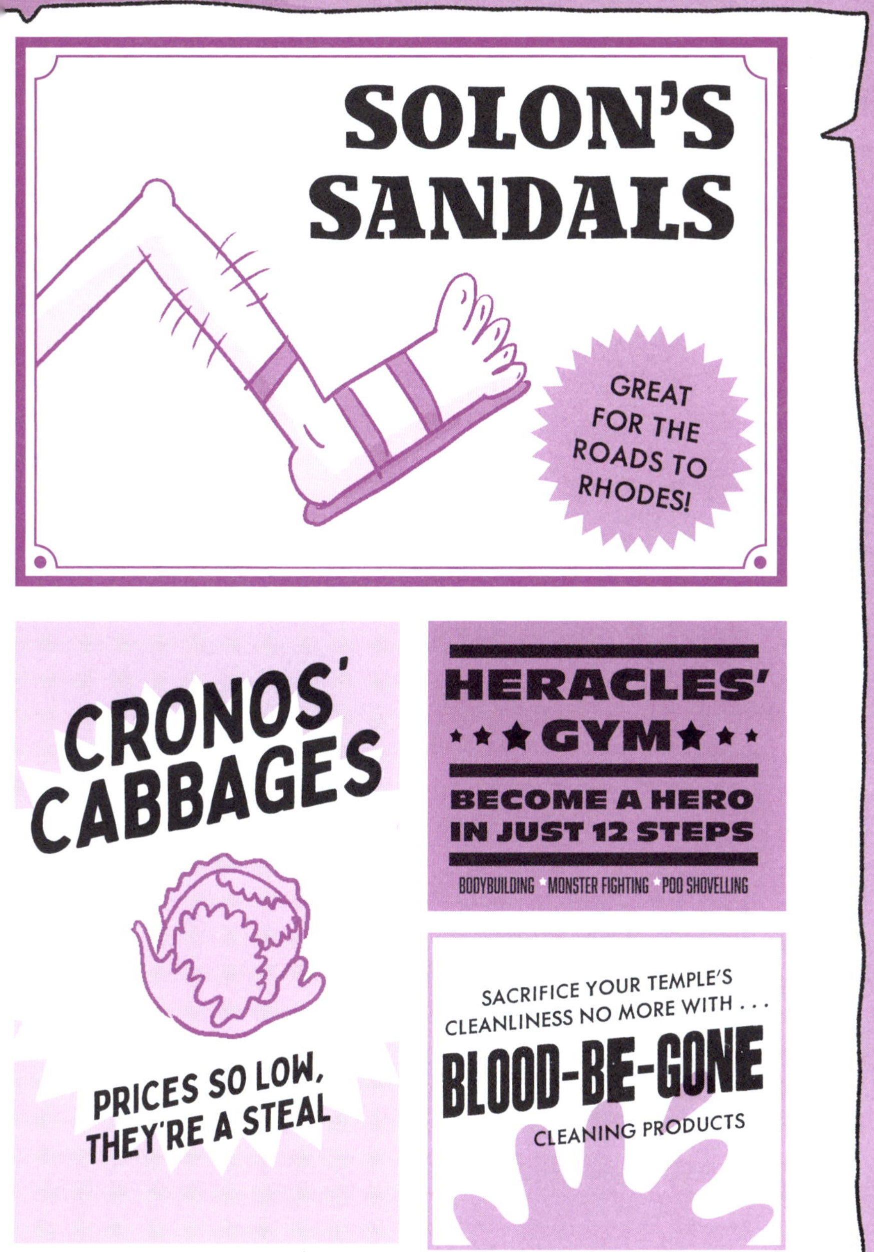
SOLON'S SANDALS
GREAT FOR THE ROADS TO RHODES!
CRONOS' CABBAGES
PRICES SO LOW, THEY'RE A STEAL
HERACLES' GYM
BECOME A HERO IN JUST 12 STEPS
BODYBUILDING * MONSTER FIGHTING * POO SHOVELLING
SACRIFICE YOUR TEMPLE'S CLEANLINESS NO MORE WITH . . .
BLOOD-BE-GONE
CLEANING PRODUCTS

FINISH HERACLES' TASKS

This famous character from Greek mythology was the son of Zeus, and an impressive hero!

Worst enemy

Hera (Zeus' wife) had it in for Heracles because his mother was another woman, which made her furious and she made Heracles go mad and kill his own wife and children.

The Labours of Heracles

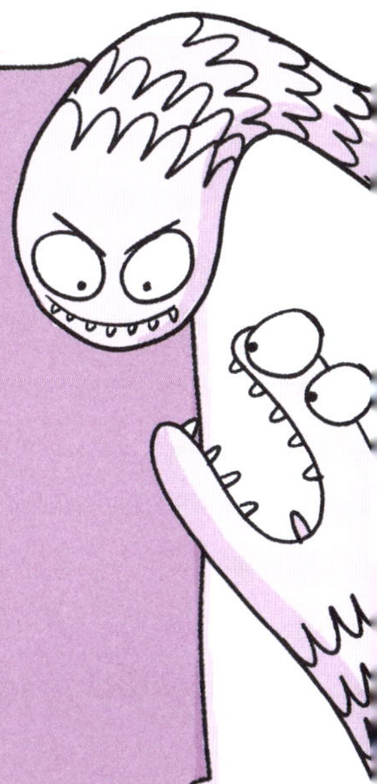

Hera's nasty plotting led to Heracles having to do a series of extremely difficult tasks as a punishment for killing his family. This involved a lot of fighting. Heracles had to . . .

1. Slay the giant, fierce Nemean lion.

2. Kill the Lernaean Hydra.

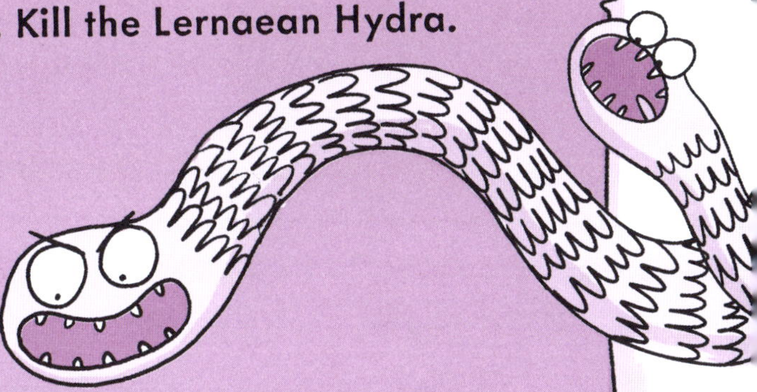

3. Capture the Ceryneian hind.

4. Capture the Erymanthian boar.

5. Clean the huge stables of King Augeas in a single day.

6. Defeat the man-eating Stymphalian birds.

7. Capture the Cretan bull.

8. Steal the mares (female horses) of King Diomedes.

9. Steal the belt of Hippolyte, queen of the Amazons.

10. Steal the cattle of the giant, Geryon.

11. Steal apples from the gardens of the Hesperides.

12. Bring back the three-headed dog Cerberus from the Underworld.

Phew! You'd think he'd need a sit down after all that . . . but some myths say he went off adventuring again with another hero, called Jason.

Get thinking

These tasks needed huge strength, but Heracles also needed to exercise his brain. To clean the stables, he built a dam to divert a river to wash away the mountains of muck. The stables were said to hold 3,000 cattle and hadn't been cleaned out for 30 years. Imagine the mess!

COULD YOU FINISH ALL OF HERACLES' TASKS?

YES!

Impressive! Go to **page 74** to meet another Greek hero, Odysseus.

NO!

Never mind. Go to **page 80** to create your own myth.

TAKE PART IN THE *PANKRATION*

Are you feeling strong? It's time for an extra-dangerous wrestling match!

The game

Pankration was a truly no-holds-barred punch-up that became a sport at the ancient Olympic games in 648BCE. It was (more or less) a combination of wrestling and boxing. You won your bout when your opponent was knocked out – or had given up!

Champion wrestler Sostratos of Sicyon's signature move was breaking his opponents' fingers!

The rules

1. No biting.
2. No eye gouging.
3. No punches or kicks to the groin.
4. Er, that's about it.

Who knew?

A referee would be on hand to hit wrestlers with a stick or whip if they broke the rules!

COULD YOU GET THROUGH THIS WRESTLING MATCH?

YES!

Impressive! Turn to **page 86** for another tough physical challenge.

NO!

How about some philosophy instead? Go back to **page 50**.

VISIT THE UNDERWORLD

Ancient Greeks believed that when a person died, they would travel to a place beneath Earth's surface. Are you ready for a trip?

The journey

The Underworld was ruled by the god Hades. Travelling there involved being taken across the mythical River Styx by a ferryman called Charon.

There was a fee for the Underworld ferry service, so the dead would be buried with a coin under their tongue.

How to be like Hades

- Wear black clothing.
- Ride a chariot drawn by black horses.
- Hang out with a three-headed dog called Cerberus.

Who knew?

Hades had a special helmet that made the wearer invisible!

COULD YOU SURVIVE A TRIP TO THE UNDERWORLD?

YES!

Some heroes managed it too, including Heracles – meet him on **page 66**.

NO!

Visit Circe's island instead. Go to **page 84**.

SAIL WITH ODYSSEUS

This Greek hero was known for being cunning and crafty.

A long journey

In mythology, Odysseus' journey home from fighting in the Trojan war took ten years! The ancient Greek poet Homer wrote all about it in his epic poem, *The Odyssey*.

Cyclops' cave

To escape from an angry cyclops (a one-eyed giant), Odysseus and his crew blinded the giant and clung to some sheep. When the cyclops reached down to feel for the men, he felt only the sheeps' woolly backs.

Sirens' song

Sirens are mythical sea creatures with voices sweet enough to lure sailors towards them – where they would drown in the dangerous water. Odysseus escaped them by tying himself to his ship's mast – he could sail past unharmed, and still hear their music!

COULD YOU SURVIVE A SEA VOYAGE WITH ODYSSEUS?

YES!

Visit Circe's island on your way – go to **page 84**.

NO!

Turn to **page 76** to go to Athens instead.

RUN AN ATHENIAN HOME

Life for women looked very different around ancient Greece – let's step into an Athenian home.

The good bits

You'd get to spend lots of time at home with your children. Women could also attend some fun ancient Greek festivals.

The bad bits

Here, women came second to men. They couldn't vote, own land or go to school, and most were married by 15 years old. Wealthier women weren't even allowed to go out shopping – they sent their slaves to do it for them!

To do list

- Looking after children
- Cooking
- Cleaning
- Weaving
- Fetching water
- Washing
- Tending to farm animals (if you had any)

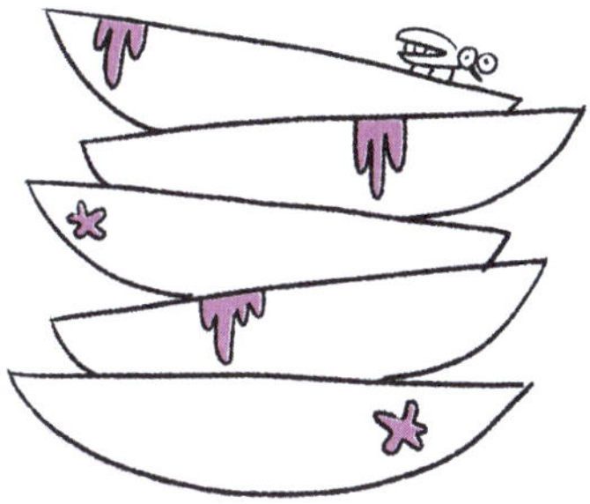

WOULD YOU SURVIVE AS AN ATHENIAN WOMEN?

YES!

Take a break from housework to meet a goddess of the home. Go back to **page 48**.

NO!

How about meeting a powerful mythological woman? Go to **page 78**.

FACE MEDUSA

This impressive character was one of the Gorgons – three sisters with live snakes for hair!

Special skills

Medusa had a scary superpower – she could turn people into stone with just a single look!

Worst enemy

The goddess Athena. Medusa started life as a beautiful woman – her hair was turned into snakes by Athena, when the goddess got angry with Medusa.

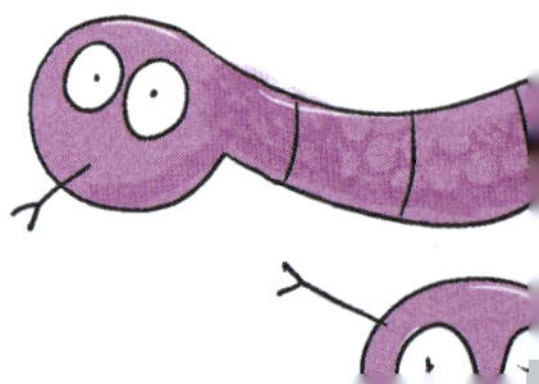

A sticky end

Medusa really couldn't catch a break. A young man called Perseus was sent to kill her – he chopped off her head and used it as a weapon to turn other people to stone.

WOULD SNAKE-HAIRED MEDUSA SCARE YOU?

YES!
Eek – try some soothing Greek crafts on **page 100**.

NO!
Meet another fierce woman from Greek mythology on **page 84**.

BUILD YOUR OWN MYTH

Pick one from each of these sections to create your very own myth! You can even name your characters or write your myth as a full story if you'd like.

Who is your hero?

1. A young prince
2. A talented craftsperson
3. A powerful sorceress
4. A goddess disguised as a human

What are they looking for?

1. Fame and glory
2. Trouble
3. Work
4. A new home

Who do they trust?

1. An oracle
2. Their loyal dog
3. The crew of their ship
4. No one

Who is their enemy?

1. An enormous sea monster
2. Zeus, king of the gods
3. Their little sister
4. A group of forest nymphs

How does their story end?

1. They are killed by their mortal enemy!
2. They get trapped on a desert island.
3. They live a long life as ruler of their city.
4. They create incredible inventions.

For even more mythology, go to **page 94** – or turn to **page 82** to continue your adventure.

JOB VACANCY

TRADER

JOB DESCRIPTION

Traders would need to be up at dawn, haggling furiously with merchants or farmers to buy goods. They would then take them to their market stall, lay them out, wait for buyers to arrive – then sell them on at a higher price!

PERKS OF THE JOB

- You'd get to spend time in the busy, vibrant agora – a big open square or area found in the middle of Greek towns.

DOWNSIDES

- You'd need to watch out for the *metronomoi* – officials employed by the city to keep an eye on the traders.
- If traders were caught cheating their customers, they would get a fine, or even be given a whipping!

WOULD YOU MAKE IT AS A TRADER?

YES! Enjoy your social time in the marketplace! You might even bump into Socrates. Go to **page 50**.

NO! Not to worry – go to **page 14** to start again.

SNEAKY BUSINESS

Some shady traders would weigh items with false scales, so their customer got less than they paid for. Mean!

TAKE ON CIRCE

It was best to keep on the good side of this skilful sorceress!

Island life

Circe was known for her magical talents – especially using herbs for potions. She lived alone on the island of Aeaea (say 'ay-EE-yah'), after being sent there by her father.

Tame lions and wolves prowled around Circe's home – perhaps humans she had transformed!

Animal magic

When the Greek hero Odysseus visited her island with his crew, Circe turned them into pigs! Odysseus escaped this fate . . . but only because the god Hermes gave him a special herb to protect him.

COULD YOU ESCAPE CIRCE'S MAGIC?

YES!
Want to weave your own mythological magic, just like Circe? Go to **page 80**.

NO!
Uh oh. Is this the end of your adventure? Go to **page 114**.

SAIL A *TRIREME*

A *trireme* was a huge 35m-long warship used in ancient Greece. Let's set sail . . .

Job description

Rowing – lots and lots of rowing. You'd spend hours heaving heavy wooden oars to propel the boat forward.

Perks of the job

You'd get to spend lots of time at sea – plus you'd have lots of other sailors to hang out with, so it would be quite social. If you could catch your breath enough to chat between strokes!

***Trireme* means 'three rows'. Every ship had three banks of oars stacked on top of each other – that's about 170 rowers!**

Drawbacks of the job

- The threat of flaming arrows setting your ship alight.
- If enemy attacks didn't get you, the unpredictable and sometimes stormy seas might!

WOULD YOU SURVIVE ON A *TRIREME*?

YES!

You must be hungry after all that rowing. Go to **page 112** for a snack.

NO!

Oops! Your ship has sunk – go to **page 114**.

BE A MATHS WHIZZ

Would you survive as a Greek mathematician?

Ask an expert . . .

ARCHIMEDES

BORN: 287BCE, Syracuse

OCCUPATION: Mathematician

FACT FILE

- Archimedes was known for wrestling with tricky maths problems! He was the first to fully understand how levers work.
- He died when Syracuse was captured by Roman soliders around 212BCE. He is said to have been so busy doing maths that he asked his killers not to disturb him! He died at around age 75, a long life for the time.

What did he do?

He worked out how to measure the volume of an odd-shaped object in water by seeing how much water it pushed away (displaced).

Archimedes is said to have made his discovery about volume in the bath – then run down the street naked!

WOULD YOU SURVIVE DOING ANCIENT GREEK SUMS?

YES!

Like the sound of a life of maths? Do you like science too? Turn to **page 106** to meet Thales.

NO!

Are other subjects more your thing? Meet Aristotle on **page 102**.

BREAK A CODE

There were many wars in ancient Greece – sending coded messages could be vital to survive. Try this tool to help . . .

Scytale

The *scytale* was a long strip of parchment or leather wound around a wooden rod. The strip had a message written on it – when unwound, the message looked like nonsense, but when it was wrapped on the stick, the words became clear. Try making your own!

Ancient messages

The *scytale* was used to carry secret messages during the Peloponnesian War – won by an army led by the city-state of Sparta.

Make a *scytale*

1. Find a long, thin strip of paper and the inside tube from a kitchen roll. Tape one end of the strip to one end of the tube.

2. Wind the paper around the roll in a coil so that the edges of the paper strip meet (or just overlap a tiny bit).

3. When the paper is fully wound, write your message onto the paper, along the length of the cylinder (like in the picture on **page 90**).

4. Unwind the paper. Now try to read it. Does it look all jumbled up? Great! You have your secret message.

5. Give it to someone else. They can decode the message by winding the paper around their own kitchen roll tube (just make sure the tube is the same size as yours).

Turn the page to try some code-cracking for yourself.

CIPHER SOLVERS

You've mastered the *scytale* – now try decoding this message! Hint: it has an ancient Greek theme . . .

VSDUWD LV

VXSHU

VWLQNB

Instructions and clues

Each letter has been shifted forward in the alphabet by a certain number – if the shift was 4, A becomes E, B becomes F, C becomes G and so on, until Z becomes D.

To check your answer, turn this page upside down.

Answer this question to find the number to shift:

How many pigs are pictured on **page 85**?

DID YOU SOLVE THE CODE?

YES!

Well done! Go back to **page 62** to meet the god of messages.

NO!

Never mind. How about trying some Greek crafts? Go to **page 104**.

ANSWER: SPARTA IS SUPER STINKY

BATTLE WITH ACHILLES

This hero was known as the greatest Greek warrior!

Early life

Achilles was the son of Peleus, a king, and Thetis, a sea goddess. He was known for being super strong, but he did have one weakness . . .

. . . his heel. Thetis dipped baby Achilles in the magical River Styx to make him invincible, but she held him by the heel to do so, leaving it unprotected.

In Greek myth, Achilles was said to have been one of the main fighters in the Trojan War.

End of a hero

Unfortunately, Achilles' heel was his downfall. He died after an arrow hit him in this unprotected area.

COULD YOU SURVIVE AGAINST ACHILLES?

YES!
Phew, that must have been hard work! Reward yourself with a snack on **page 112**.

NO!
Oh dear! Go to **page 114**.

BE A THINKER

Want to solve some thorny Greek problems?

PYTHAGORAS

BORN: 570BCE, Samos

OCCUPATION: Mathematician, philosopher

FACT FILE

- Pythagoras was the first to use maths to describe and explain the world!
- He discovered rules about triangles and ratios, and explained music with maths.
- He was one of the first to suggest that the Earth is ball-shaped, not flat.
- Pythagoras believed that beans have souls, so shouldn't be eaten.

The Pythagoreans

Pythagoras was so popular that he had a group of followers – they had strange customs, such as always putting on their right sandal first and never going for a wee whilst facing the Sun.

WOULD YOU THRIVE AS A GREEK THINKER?

YES!

If you can't get enough of maths, go to **page 106**.

NO!

Prefer working with your hands? Turn to **page 104**.

STEAL CABBAGES

Would you do anything to get one of your five-a-day? Let's get stuck in!

Job description

Steal as many cabbages as you can . . . without getting caught.

Pros and cons

True, you'd get free food . . . but it could end badly. Around 621 BCE, an early Greek ruler, Draco, gave the death penalty to thieves, even if they had just stolen a single measly cabbage. *Gulp!*

Draco's Punishment Menu for Thieves

- Throw them off a cliff/ down a deep pit.
- Tie them to a board and leave them for wild animals to find.
- Give them poison to drink.

Who knew?

Some poor ancient Greeks didn't have much choice in the matter. If they had no money, stealing food was the only way to eat, however risky it was!

COULD YOU LAST AS A THIEF?

YES!
Sneaky! Go to **page 116**.

NO!
Eek, it's not looking good. Go to **page 114**.

DESIGN A GREEK VASE

Ancient Greek pottery is famous for its beautiful designs – many feature stories from mythology. How about designing your own vase? Copy the shape opposite onto a separate piece of paper and decorate it however you like.

Pattern ideas

- Waves
- Leaves
- Zig-zags
- Flowers

Design ideas

- Your family, friends or teachers
- Your pets
- Wild animals
- Monsters

Could you see yourself as a Greek craftsperson? If so, turn to **page 104.** If not, turn to **page 102** to continue your adventure.

BE A SCHOLAR

Think a scholar's life might be for you?

Ask an expert . . .

ARISTOTLE

BORN: 384BCE, Stagira

OCCUPATION: Philosopher, scientist – and more!

FACT FILE

- Aristotle was the first to classify living things into groups, and he invented types of logical reasoning. His work is still influencing thinkers today – not too shabby!
- Many of his works have not survived – we only have around one fifth of them today.
- Aristotle was personal tutor to Alexander the Great, who went on to be a successful leader.

Animal magic

Aristotle believed that eels didn't reproduce – they just appeared out of mud!

Aristotle spent a lot of time studying animals. He documented over 500 different species!

COULD YOU FLOURISH AS A GREEK SCHOLAR?

YES!

For more great Greek ideas, meet Thales on **page 106**.

NO!

Turn to **page 104** to try something more practical.

JOB VACANCY

CRAFT WORKER

JOB DESCRIPTION
Get really good at your craft – then sell your wares!

PERKS OF THE JOB
You could end up famous. One ancient Greek potter called Exekias was well-known for his super-fancy pots. He even signed some of them, like artists today.

DOWNSIDES
It could be hard work – some wealthier Greeks grew rich using slaves to make goods for them. In Athens, Cephalus owned a factory where 120 slaves made shields to sell. Even if they weren't slaves, some ancient Greek craft workers were looked down on by upper-class people.

CRAFTS TO PICK
- Pottery
- Carpentry
- Weaving
- Leatherworking
- Metalworking

INSPIRATION

Many ancient Greek objects, such as drinking vessels, included images of stories from mythology.

WOULD YOU MAKE IT AS A CRAFT WORKER?

YES!

How about some lunch after all that hard work? Turn to **page 112**.

NO!

Not to worry – go to **page 14** to start again.

HELP ME FIND MY HUSBAND

MISSING

ODYSSEUS

LAST SEEN SAILING BY THE ISLE OF AEAEA.
IF FOUND, PLEASE CONTACT PENELOPE.

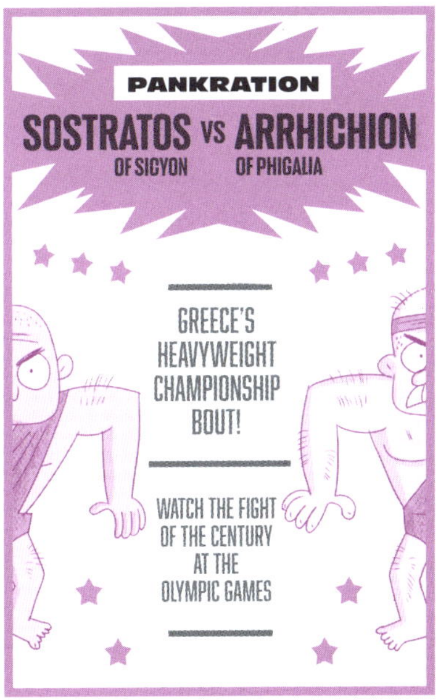

BE AN ASTRONOMER

Would you love to study the stars?

Ask an expert . . .

THALES OF MILETUS

BORN: 624–620BCE, Miletus

OCCUPATION: Philosopher, scientist, astronomer

FACT FILE

- Thales used science rather than myths to explain the world.
- He was the first person to predict a solar eclipse (when the Moon blocks out all light from the Sun).
- It's believed that he was once so deep in thought that he accidentally walked into a well. Ouch!

Maths whizz

Thales learned how to measure the heights of things just by using angles and the length of the shadows they cast.

WOULD YOU MAKE IT AS A GREEK ASTRONOMER?

YES!

You've used your super brains to survive ancient Greece!
Go to **page 116**.

NO!

There are plenty more options to try. Go to **page 14** to start again.

WRITE A PLAY

Fancy trying your hand at some Greek theatre?

AESCHYLUS

BORN: 525–524BCE, Gela

OCCUPATION: Playwright

FACT FILE

- Aeschylus was the first known writer of Greek tragedies – plays that didn't end well for one (or more) of the main characters.
- Many of his characters were famous figures from Greek mythology.
- He wrote more than 70 plays during his lifetime – but only seven complete ones have survived for us to enjoy today.

A *turtle* disaster

Around 455BCE, an eagle was said to have dropped a tortoise it had caught straight onto Aeschylus' head. It had mistaken him for a rock! The blow from the hard shell killed him instantly.

WOULD YOU BE GREAT AS A GREEK PLAYWRIGHT?

YES!

Try out some real-life creative writing on **page 80**.

NO!

It's the end of the ancient Greek road for you. Go to **page 114**.

WORSHIP APHRODITE

Get ready to meet the goddess of love. Be careful – she could be harsh!

Character traits

Charming and charismatic – sometimes vain. She could make people fall in love in a heartbeat . . . but anyone who insulted her could expect punishment!

Worst enemy

Aphrodite clashed with Zeus' wife, Hera, who was envious of her beauty. The two goddesses also supported opposite sides in the Trojan war – Aphrodite backed the Trojans, Hera the Greeks.

Aphrodite was associated with many birds, including doves, swans and sparrows.

Who knew?

In one myth, Aphrodite was said to have cursed a group of women who failed to worship her. The curse gave the women a dreadful smell!

Specialist subjects

- Love
- Fertility
- Beauty

COULD YOU HAVE STAYED ON APHRODITE'S GOOD SIDE?

YES!

Well done! Fancy another challenge? Go back to **page 32** to meet another goddess.

NO!

Ask Hermes for help – go back to **page 62**.

EAT LIKE A GREEK

Can you make it through an ancient Greek meal? Pick your favourites from this menu of specialities . . .

BREAKFAST

Other common foods included dried and salted fish, olives, and nuts such as walnuts and almonds.

Flatbread

This was often dipped in wine and served with a few figs or olives. No cornflakes, sorry!

DRINK

Kykeon

This early smoothie was a sludgy mix containing barley, goats' cheese, water and herbs!

LUNCH AND DINNER

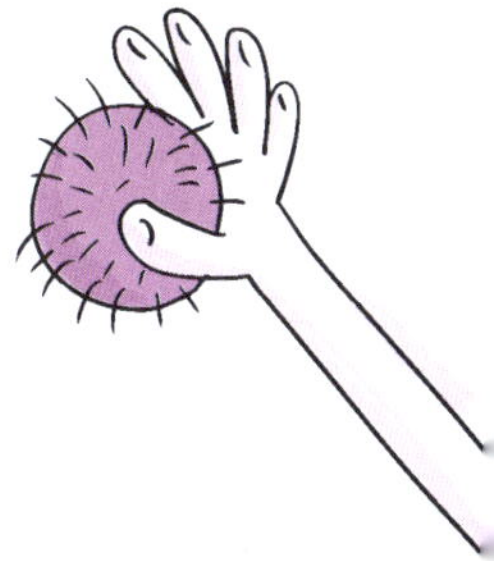

Sea urchins

These spiky sea creatures were caught by hand (ouch!), covered in mud and baked.

Black soup

This Spartan broth was made of boiled pigs' legs and plenty of pigs' blood. The only other flavourings were salt and vinegar!

Stew

Many Greeks ate plenty of barley, lentils, peas and beans. Farts ahoy!

Pelican pie

Most Greeks didn't eat much red meat . . . but they did chomp on birds such as sparrows, swans and pelicans.

COULD YOU STOMACH AN ANCIENT GREEK MEAL?

YES!

If your food has given you energy for more challenges, go to **page 14** to start again.

NO!

Turn to **page 114** to finish.

OOPS!

You didn't survive this time!

Life in ancient Greece could be difficult. As you've found out, many Greeks ended up in risky situations such as fighting in wars, getting on the wrong side of the law or falling out with gods. Even heroes in Greek mythology weren't invincible and could meet with a sticky end.

Fancy another go at ancient Greek life? Go back to page 14 to start your adventure all over again . . .

HOORAY!

YOU SURVIVED ANCIENT GREECE! Your brilliant choices have led you to lead a happy life in this amazing ancient world – congratulations!

You can end your adventure here – or to find out even more ancient Greek facts, go back to to page 14 to start all over again. Will you be as lucky the next time?

Pssst – want to find out how the ancient Greek civilization came to an end? Turn to page **118** – or turn to page **120** for a quiz.

THE END OF ANCIENT GREECE!

You've tried out life in ancient Greece and discovered the fun – and difficulties – they had. But how did this incredible civilization come to an end?

With there being so many city-states in ancient Greece, conflict was common. Decades of wars between city-states in the fourth century BCE had left them weak and ripe for invasion. In 338BCE, Philip II of Macedon, Greece's northern neighbour, conquered Thebes and Athens. When Philip died, his son, Alexander the Great, took over and built the powerful Macedonian Empire, stretching from Greece into Asia.

When Alexander died suddenly in 323BCE, a mega struggle for power saw his brief empire split into multiple mini empires. These were later conquered by Roman forces who were big fans of the Greeks. The Romans were real copycats and borrowed many Greek ideas, customs, architectural styles and even their gods. By doing this, they have helped keep our knowledge of the amazing ancient Greeks alive. Their history, myths, inventions and philosophy are all still popular today, thousands of years later.

QUIZ

Can you answer these five questions about ancient Greece, using all the amazing facts you've discovered?

1. Who was the ancient Greek god of the sea?

a) Zeus

b) Poseidon

c) Hermes

2. How many heads did Cerberus (the mythological guardian dog of the Underworld) have?

a) Three

b) Ten

c) One hundred

3. Most ancient Greek athletes competed in the Olympic games naked.

True or false?

4. In which ancient Greek city-state did women often practise lots of physical exercise, such as running and wrestling?

a) Athens

b) Corinth

c) Sparta

5. Some ancient Greek plays could last all day.

True or false?

Answers: 1. b, 2. a, 3. True, 4. c, 5. True

ABOUT THE AUTHOR

Clive Gifford has travelled through many parts of the ancient Greek world. He's seen temples in Rhodes, Crete and Attica, clambered up the Acropolis in Athens and stood, ready to race, on the start line of the track at the famous ancient Olympia stadium. Clive has written more than 200 books and has won the Royal Society, SLA and Blue Peter book awards. He lives in Manchester, UK.

ABOUT THE ILLUSTRATOR

As a young boy, Tim Wesson was constantly doodling, finding any excuse to put pen to paper. Since turning his much-loved pastime into his profession, Tim has achieved great success in the world of children's publishing, having illustrated and authored books across a variety of formats. He takes great delight in turning the world on its head and inviting children to go on the adventure with him.

GET READY FOR MORE HILARIOUS ANCIENT ANTICS IN THE NEXT *YOU PICK HISTORY* BOOK.